AF268535

To my parents, who sat with me at the dining room table, gluing dreams to paper when I was just six years old. Your belief in me planted the seed for this book.

To my partner, whose unwavering support inspires me every day, and to all my friends and family who light my path—thank you for believing in me.

And to every reader: Believe in yourself, but never underestimate your power to help others believe in themselves too. Share your light, and watch the world grow brighter.

First published in Canada by
All Three Publishing Inc., 2024

www.allthree.ca

Text copyright © Maggie Larocque
Illustration copyright © Jimmy Vu
www.byjimmyvu.ca
Book Design by Jimmy Vu in consultation with Maggie Larocque

ISBN: 978-1-7387579-1-6

Printed in Canada

MR. ANT'S MAGIC PANTS

BY Maggie Larocque

PICTURES BY JIMMY VU

All Three Publishing

In a bustling ant colony beneath a big oak tree,
Lived a tiny ant named Andy, as shy as can be.
While other ants marched in lines so neat,
Andy felt different, incomplete.

#1
STRONG
-DUDE-

"I'm not strong like Sam
or smart like Sue,
What good am I?
What can I do?"
Andy sighed
as he watched his friends,
Carrying crumbs and leaves,
making amends.

5

One day, while exploring a human picnic site,
Andy spotted something shiny and bright.
A tiny pair of pants, sparkling blue,
"I wonder," thought Andy, "what these can do?"

He slipped them on, a perfect fit!
Suddenly, Andy felt strong and full of grit.
He lifted a cookie crumb, big as could be,
"Wow!" he exclaimed, "Is this really me?"

9

Back at the colony, the Queen was distressed,
"Our food supply is low, we're all so stressed!"
Andy, feeling brave in his new magic pants,
Declared, "I'll find food! I'll take the chance!"

The other ants gasped, "But Andy, it's too far!
Many have tried and failed to reach the jar!"
But Andy just smiled and said with a wink,
"With these magic pants, I can do anything, I think!"

12

Off he went on his dangerous quest,
To find the fabled jar, he'd do his best.
He crossed puddles wide and grass so tall,
His magic pants helping him through it all.

A hungry bird swooped down for a snack,
But Andy's pants gave him the power to fight back.
He tickled its beak and made it sneeze,
Then scurried away through the leaves with ease.

At last, he reached the giant glass jar,
Filled with sweet treats from near and far.
But as he stretched to reach the rim so high,
His magic pants ripped with a cry!

18

Oh no!" cried Andy, "My pants are torn!
How will I get home? I feel so forlorn!"
But then he remembered all he'd done,
The challenges faced, the battles won.

With determination in his tiny heart,
Andy knew it was time to make a new start.
He climbed that jar with his own six feet,
And gathered the food, oh what a feat!

22

The journey home was long and tough,
But Andy discovered he was more than enough.
He used his smarts to avoid the rain,
And his strength to carry the sugary grain.

When Andy returned, the colony cheered,
"You've saved us all!" they happily peered.
Andy smiled and said,
"I thought I needed magic to be strong,
But the power was inside me all along!"

27

From that day on, Andy walked tall and proud,
He believed in himself and stood out from the crowd.
He learned that magic isn't in what you wear,
But in believing in yourself and the courage to dare.

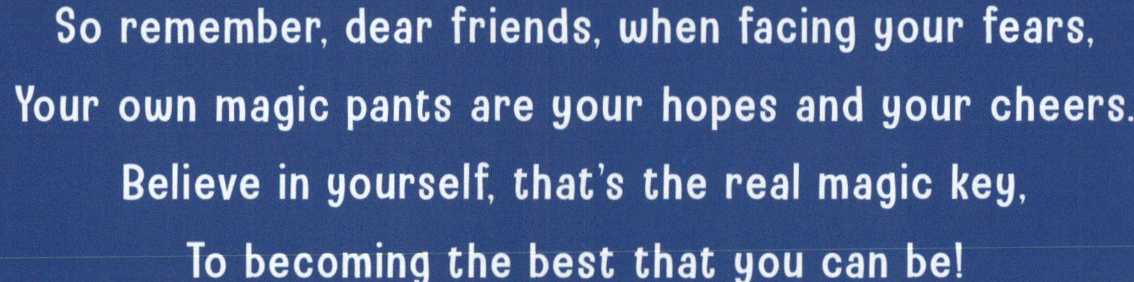

So remember, dear friends, when facing your fears,
Your own magic pants are your hopes and your cheers.
Believe in yourself, that's the real magic key,
To becoming the best that you can be!

30

Maggie Larocque

Maggie Larocque first penned the whimsical tale of "Mr. Ant's Magic Pants" at the young age of 6 proving that creativity knows no age limit. Now, with 24 years of life experience and nearly two university degrees under her belt (or should we say, magic pants?), she has revisited this cherished story, infusing it with newfound depth and meaning.

As a dedicated professional in the nonprofit sector, Maggie spends her days mentoring children aged 6-12, during which she is constantly inspired by their boundless curiosity, infectious excitement, and zest for life. However, her work has also revealed a sobering truth: many children grapple with self-doubt and a lack of confidence. This realization became the catalyst for revamping Mr. Ant's Magic Pants. Maggie recognized that the book's message of inner strength, grit, and self-belief resonates not only with young readers but with individuals of all ages. Through her writing, she aims to nurture the seeds of self-assurance in both children and adults alike, reminding us all: our greatest magic lies within. With a delightful blend of humor, heart, and a dash of ant-sized wisdom, Maggie invites readers to slip on their own pair of magic pants and embark on a journey of self-discovery. After all, as Mr. Ant would surely agree, sometimes the smallest creatures can teach us the biggest lessons.